It's a Job, not Work

Tiffany Thompson

ISBN: 978-1-7370465-1-6

It's a Job, Not Work

Proudly self-published through Divine Legacy Publishing, www.divinelegacypublishing.com

Dedication

I dedicate this book to all those seeking work. I pray that God/The Universe connects you to your divine purpose.

Author's Notes

Thank you so much for purchasing it's a *Job, Not Work*. I pray that this book encourages you and enriches your life as much as it did for me. When I wrote this book, I was going through a challenging and dark time in my life. I was looking for some inspiration, and I was inclined to find it for myself. I hope that my journey in discovering my work makes your journey easier.

Although a lot has changed since I wrote this book eleven years ago, it is so relevant even today. When I wrote this book, I had no clue that everything that has transpired would occur. While in the thick of it, I was challenged, but I knew there was a light at the end of the tunnel.

The light is brighter than I could have ever imagined. Since writing this book, I have obtained my school counseling and mental health license. In addition, I've written five other books, started a successful podcast with some friends called Four Tribe Society, and I'm a few months away from obtaining my doctorate in Expressive Therapies. I also write a monthly article for a teen magazine called BoldlyU, and I started my counseling, coaching, and consulting business called Cre8tive Recovery, LLC.

I write these things not to boast but to share with you that you too can accomplish every goal you could imagine. Do not allow the nights and cold evenings to take your joy. You have everything within you. You are equipped with purpose. I'm a firm believer in finding your daily ritual and sticking to a plan. Be mindful of who you are giving gratitude to and focus on your heart. Continuously tap into love, and you will never go wrong on this journey called life. It sounds taboo, but truly stop each day, smell the roses, and realize that life is full of adventure. You have to get on board and ride out God's plan for your life. It is effortless!

The Beginning of the Journey from My Job to My Work

After being fired or laid off from a job, you wonder, what's next for me? I can tell you, for me it was an exhausting up and down roller coaster. I first felt anger, shame, revenge, and pity, but somewhere between the anger and pity, I found peace. Yes, I said peace. It's hard to think that one can find peace when they're placed in such an unpleasant situation. However, I was able to grasp it, hold onto it, and accept it.

Now, don't get me wrong, peace came and went. There were some days that I felt great amounts of peace and joy. It was on those days that I enjoyed the ability to spend the extra free time with my kids. It was nice to sleep in during the week, if I chose to, and to have the freedom to be at home and cook dinner as I anticipated the arrival of my husband from work.

It's funny because I was on Facebook one day and a Facebook friend of mine posted a video of Pastor Jamal Bryant preaching that a "job was from the devil." He stated, "God had never intended on us having a job." This sermon was confirmation for me. For years I had jokingly told myself that a job had to be from the enemy, because it appeared to consume so much of our lives. In my opinion, jobs seemed to keep us from truly being "free." Pastor Bryant went on to speak about how a "job" was never mentioned in the Bible and that God had only intended for us to "work."

At first, this concept did not fully register with me-- then it hit me. I realized that for years I had been praying wrong. I had been praying for jobs and interviews. It had been 16 months since I'd had my last full time job. I had been on several interviews, but I was not making the cut. This wore on my self-esteem and self-worth. I started to feel as though I was useless and incompetent. It's funny how the devil will play on our emotions, and he was having a field day with mine. I had lost my job due to lies and discrimination and was in the midst of a lawsuit against my former employer. I was so beaten and hurt. I was disappointed and frustrated, and I even started to get mad at God. I had little faith and no hope.

That's why when the Facebook post came across my computer--it hit me! I thought back to all my past job experiences, how it would always start off so great and the money would get better and better--yet eventually I would come to a place where I would either become

2

complacent, the job would not fulfill me, or management would try to find an illusion of what was not right about me in the position.

I thought about how I would give so much time to these jobs and how I would work so diligently to be the best employee. I would put in late hours and early mornings trying to be successful, and many times I was not appreciated and underdeveloped in my role. I soon realized I was just a replaceable asset, nothing more than a doll or a toy. The company was the kid and I was the new present; once I started to get old, used, and worn they would grow bored and decide to get rid of me. I was expunged.

It's ridiculous that we are just a part of the bottom line these days. And most of us don't even realize that we are just an expense that can be replaced or cut. It's sad that our society does not give value and worth to its most valuable asset--its people.

I learned this the hard way when my family went through a difficult situation with my son's health. While unemployed, I had time to sit and think about how many times my child, who at the time suffered from a seizure disorder and chronic asthma, would be in the hospital sick. However, because management would be on a power trip, and I was afraid of a write up or termination, I was unable to leave and be with him.

I thought about all the miserable things that occurred to me while on a "job." It was at that moment I realized I had been living life all wrong. I realized God had so much more for me than a "job." I knew at that moment my calling was bigger; He had an assignment for me. He had an opportunity, and He had work that He needed to be done.

I always wanted to write a book to inspire others, and as I listened to Pastor Bryant talk about how God had work for us to do, I realized that I had not been doing God's work, but that I had been doing the devil's job. When I realized that what I had been focusing on was all wrong, I started to pray and ask God to forgive me and to help me see more clearly the work He would have me do.

It was at that moment that I knew my work was not to go to a job at a company and that I was never put on this earth to have a job. I, like all of you, was placed on this earth to work. We all have been given many talents, something we can offer in exchange for a meaningful life. My life had been so incomplete up until that moment. Even as I rejoiced in my knowledge, I still was not satisfied. Because, as they say, "knowing is only half the battle." The real challenge was discovering what this work was.

We all like to think that we have the answers. However, I'm the first to admit that I know nothing and have very few answers. I just pray daily, weekly, and monthly for wisdom and knowledge. I ask God to give me wisdom so that as I obtain knowledge, I know what to do with it. It was this prayer that came to my mind as I went through this difficult and challenging situation with my employment. Nevertheless, what appeared to be the most difficult and challenging circumstance became the best situation.

Although it was apparent that I was lost, it was ironic because I thought I had found myself. I knew I had found something when I came to the realization that I was not placed here to do a job. But again, what was the work God placed me here to do?

I sat and waited, pondered, stressed, and tried to figure this out in my mind. I even asked others what their thoughts were on career choices for me. I contemplated being an attorney, a schoolteacher, going back to banking, and I even dreamed about doing fundraising again.

I tried to do several businesses, both on my own and with partners, but somehow even with my passion behind it--something happened. I'd start looking for a job, they'd start looking for a job, or I'd put it on the back burner because of lack of funds or common visions.

Becoming your own boss requires lots of money, and when you're unemployed with bad credit and bad money habits, it's hard to start a business. Plus, my focus was unclear, and I had no direction. I picked up a part time summer job teaching acting to kindergarteners for Summer Advantage USA. Jill Gildersleeve, the program director, would tell us that when she would explain new information to her students, she would ask them, "Was it clear?" and "How clear was it?" She would say to them, "So are there bugs, mud, or Windex on your window?" Many of the students would say, "I see bugs," and others would say, "It's Windex clean." She said she finally had one child bold enough to speak up and say, "My window is full of mud, and I can't seem to see anything."

For me, that was how this journey began. It started off very muddy. Some days I just saw bugs, but for the most part it was muddy, and I couldn't see anything. I'd get frustrated and try to wipe it down, but I still couldn't see clear.

Wiping my window down was me following sin and getting deeper and deeper into it. When I would decide to wipe the window, I would allow my own inner demons to take control and I put myself into situations that were not always the most righteous or "holy in thought, action, or deed. My actions would just bring confusion and that would lead to disappointment.

My husband would say, "Honey, we need to get it together and go to church more." I would hear him but something in my heart would tune him out. My heart would turn cold, and I wouldn't want to hear what he had to say. Although I was not fully listening, my spirit was, and it was reacting slowly to his voice.

It's funny because, at one point in my life, I was so wrapped up in God I would attend church faithfully. I was so consumed that I didn't even watch television or listen to music. In a blink of an eye, everything was different in my life. Somewhere on this path the direction of my journey changed. Although I enjoyed my life when I was deeply rooted in church, something about it was not real; it was incomplete, unfinished, and undone.

Somewhere along the line, church stopped being church and it became a corporation. It started to appear more like a job, and less like a place that I could come and get the word of God. The pastors all appeared to be Wall Street bookies, and I was just a lost soul trying to pay to get into heaven.

I looked at my current life and although it was not totally sold out for Christ like it had been years prior, it seemed to be a little more manageable and easier without the church pimps selling me propaganda that they didn't even live nor believe-- so I thought.

However, the realty of the situation was that both lives were unfulfilled. In both lives I found myself torn and not working. I started to think about Pastor Bryant's words, "God placed us here to work." Every time I thought about those words, chills would go down my spine. I soon noticed a pattern in me and my problem. The problem I had in my college life, my religious fanatic life, and my married life was that I had never worked. Yes, I had jobs; I held plenty of jobs in my life. I had been blessed, successful, and made some good money in many of my careers. The problem was that I had never felt complete in any of these situations and I wasn't sure if I had been working for God on these jobs.

I had not found my purpose or calling. I thought about the book *A Purpose Driven Life*. My friend Natalie, my sorority sister, had purchased a copy and given it to me for my birthday one year. Although I owned the book and heard many great things about it, I glimpsed through the pages but didn't feel the need to read it.

Now, in what felt like a purposeless life, I had second thoughts about my decision to not read the book. I sat in my thoughts looking down on my words and thinking about work. I wondered, if I had read that book whether I would have figured out my purpose. I shrugged it off and laughed at the thought.

I had always questioned how a book could give you a purpose for your life. In my eyes you could only find purpose in one book and that was the Holy Bible. I'm not a bible scholar, and I would never say that I'm this big religious fanatic--to date.

To say the least, I'm probably more of a person that just has faith, and that faith is based on Christian principles. I came to know that the Christ Spirit must be your guide and love must be the core of all relationships. I know some folks get very passionate and start to condemn those who don't believe the same as them. However, I don't get bent out of shape if others don't share my same belief. I will share my thoughts and experiences to help others get insight on how I came to know where my faith lies. I truly believe that we all need faith and something to believe in outside of ourselves.

With all that said, it still didn't explain what my work was to be or how I would even get it done. I would speak to God and say, "Okay, God, I have several college degrees, including a master's degree. I've studied everything from theater, telecommunications, business, and anthropology, and still have no clue." I would continue my conversation with God and dwell on the times I had traveled and lived abroad in Tanzania and Kenya. He would show me that I had great experiences--yet no work.

There were many times in my life that I just knew I was going to be an actress. I had it all planned; I'd move to Hollywood and it would just happen for me. Then, somewhere between turning down a contract with Elite Modeling agency, meeting my husband, and graduating college, it all changed.

Somewhere, I got a job and became confined to it. I never really loved the work that I did but was always able to find a way to have passion behind it. I'm a person of great passion--if I love it you will know it. But, at the age of 34, I sat jobless for almost two years with no passion, no desire, little faith, and no hope.

I had just watched Pastor Bryant give a sermon on jobs and work and I still could not grasp how this related to me. I knew that the sermon was *for* me, because I had just received news about a job I had interviewed for not choosing me. I felt so low, like dirt! I cried and pitied myself for a minute before my husband talked some sense into me and helped me feel better.

This had become routine in my house. I'd go for a job interview, give it my all, think it went well, and a few days later I'd get a rejection email or a call telling me I was great, but they had decided to go with another candidate. Or I'd get no response at all. I'd cry and cry and beat myself up, telling myself I was the worst person and didn't deserve to live. I'd get so bummed out and depressed, but for my husband I'd show a happy face immediately.

Deep down in my heart and soul, I was miserable. For weeks, and sometimes months, I'd feel sad. I felt like such a loser and would remember back to all the lies and mean things that were stated on my reviews out of retaliation. This made me feel worse. There were times when I wanted to drive up to the building, go in, smack the lady who betrayed my faith in mankind with her lies and manipulation, and say, "You blank, blank, blank! Don't you know I have kids? You have totally destroyed my life with your false statements! Thanks, blank."

Then reality would hit me, and God would tell me in his quiet way, "Peace, be still, this is not your battle and they did you a favor." Afterwards, I'd cry over the pain I felt. I realized that it was just a job; it was not the work that God wanted me to do.

I began to understand that my work is much bigger than what most of these companies had to offer. I also understood that part of my work was to allow these organizations to use me, hurt me, and try to tear me down so that I could truly get to work and help others find their work as well.

It became apparent that opportunities would take me into the work that God had for my life. We sometimes become so consumed with the goals we have for our lives, and what job we should take or career choice is available that we don't look for work. I know after being terminated I thought about it constantly; it consumed me. I tried hard to figure it out on my own. Trying to figure out your role in this life is a journey we must all venture into.

What is Faith?

It's awesome to see those who just know; they plan it out and it appears that everything falls in place. However, I'm friends with a lot of these people and I know they too have stories. They have stories of setbacks, failure and fear of the unknown.

I know it's so difficult to imagine that you are not alone when you're going through your test, but as I went through, and at the time of writing this book was still going through my personal test, I realized that I wasn't truly alone. I met some great people in similar situations and some whose were far worse.

The only thing that kept most of us going was our faith. I had Muslim, Christian, and Buddhist friends and some friends that I wasn't sure believed in anything but self. However, the one thing that united us all was this test of our faith. When your faith is tested you start to understand the core of the human heart and spirit. You find out where the strength of survival lies. I realized that for most of the folks I came across, it was in their faith that they were able to carry on and those who lacked the faith many times lost the battle.

I know this book is about finding work not a job, but the unique thing about this journey is that you can't find your work without discovering and uncovering your faith. You will not find your work, because it is your faith that leads you to want to work. For me, this has been a challenge, a difficult task. I would say it's probably been one of the most difficult obstacles ever placed before me.

The entire process has been overwhelming, humiliating, mind changing, and life altering. How can not having work *not* be life altering? It's something I would never wish upon my worst enemy. However, it's probably something that I would recommend to all my friends who are truly searching for their purpose in life.

I think back to when I was a teenager and how I would lay on the back of my boyfriend's car outside my parent's house. We'd look at the stars and have these deep conversations about our futures and God. Everything seemed so perfect, so simple, so easy--I thought I could and would accomplish everything we talked about. The funny thing is that "we" didn't accomplish the main thing we'd discussed: us being together forever and getting married. However, I did finally accomplish getting married and being in love, just not with him-. I found someone else who loved me as much as I loved him, and my high school sweetheart found the same in another individual.

I tell this story to say that life is like that on so many facets; we have goals and dreams, and they don't always play out the way in which we think or believe that they should. And yet, God does not forsake us, and He places us in a position that will enable us to accomplish what our hearts desire.

Although my high school sweetheart may not have been "the one," there was someone else for him and me. I know that jobs can be this way. We can sometimes get a job and just know that "This is it, it's the perfect fit." Or we can apply or interview for a position and know "This is the one."

However, that may not be the case. God is the only one that can place us into work. Just as we may think a person is "the one," God can change those plans. He can change any plan He chooses to change. He can also change the plans of our careers and future goals. That is why we must always have faith. By having faith, God is able to lead us to His desires, His wants, and His goals for our lives.

I know this can be very hard to grasp, especially when we have already planned out our destinies. God changed my plans quickly in every situation; it was like one moment I was a teenager laying on the back of, what I thought was, the love of my life's car planning my future, and the next minute I find out that God has other plans. I realize that the dreams and plans we contemplate are not always what God has in store. I use this story because in my life this had to be one of the most difficult times and, as Oprah would say, was my "aha" moment.

I always had faith, or so I thought, but my faith was based on my desires and my wants. This situation made me realize that faith does not always lead to things going the way I think they should go. This became even more real for me in this journey to find work. As I planned out whom I would marry and we planned out our careers and future, I realized that *we* did all the planning--where was God?

Oh! Yes, God was there, but he was not interested in our plans. We had already destroyed those plans by not having the right type of faith. A faith that was built upon unselfishness, not a faith that was based on our selfish desires that only involved God when we were not worshiping each other. We humans many times are selfish and sometimes put people and jobs before God. However, when you truly are seeking work--it will never come before Him because the work will always involve His presence.

I think it's funny how many times we have to learn these basic concepts in life situations that cause us to sacrifice for Him. I'm just thankful that I learned many of my lessons as a teenager. I found out that things don't always work out the way we desire or want them to work. So many people don't (and never will) understand that when you are truly living to work for God. He will bring all the pieces together and will place the people in your path that He wants to be there when you make it to that destiny.

I went through days, nights, weeks, and months trying to understand the position and placement of my life, not knowing that I had spent a lot of time looking for a job and little time preparing for the real work.

Days, weeks, and months went by and I still found myself without work. I started to get depressed and questioned the position in which God had placed me. My mind would go blank after weeks and weeks of going back and forth on job interviews and contemplating my next job moves. I'd hear the small voice in me that said, "Prepare for work, not a job," then I'd start to get anxious and scared and wonder if I would ever find what it is that God had set forth for me.

Many feelings came up against me. I pressed on in the word of God and stayed encouraged through the words of my caring, supportive husband, family and friends, and the faith they had in my abilities. Even with such a great support system that showers you in accolades of love and prayer, you have to realize the faith for yourself. This is the most difficult thing to do when you are going through the test.

You recall the Bible stories of David's life and his setbacks and accomplishments and you aspire to be more like him. You picture him going up against Goliath and taking him down with a rock. However, for you, it's the journey of looking for work that becomes your Goliath. You stand face to face with your giant and you look within yourself for the strength to get through the test and you search for the rock--the rock where your faith dwells. Every journey, every interview, every rejection, and every lonely night within your own thoughts becomes an overwhelming task. You fight with all your might not to become like Moses and strike your rock out of anger.

You wonder how you will get through it, and you want to cry and give up in the race. You hear the words that gently say to you, "The battle is not yours, it's the Lord's." These words ring into your heart and you find strength to continue to move forward. Each day you set foot into the horizon you find new things to move you and new reasons to wake up and hold onto faith. You picture the Israelites walking into the Promised Land, and you tap into the faith and hope that they had for those 40 years in confusion.

You realize that the work is only a small piece of the puzzle. You know that this journey is deeper than finding your place or your position. The journey that you are on is a journey that may lead to a deeper relationship and understanding of the God we serve, the God that has done so much for us. You recall back to all the moments in which your faith moved you to that next place. Except this time, you don't have any clue where you're headed. You're like a deer in headlights, eyes wide open and ready to jump. You don't know which way to move or turn. You go into your own mind and hope that you can find some calm, some peace. Yes, peace and calm come to you-- yet again you know that it will not be long before you have to face the reality of your circumstances.

I'm so blessed and so lucky because I have a family, and I have someone to help me in this battle--those are the words that come to comfort me in my deep thought. This may be true, but I still feel all alone, as if I have no one in this world. It's difficult to see the things around you when you are used to being proactive and involved in your destiny. When you are the one that has been in charge of making things happen around you through your dreams, visions, and plans. For the first time in your life, you cannot see clearly.

Things are all muddy and it becomes a tragedy; it appears to be an unbearable situation despite knowing that this is not the end. You don't know what is to come next. You have to rely on your faith, but the last time your faith was tested, God changed the situation so quickly. This time you feel as though you can't reach out to Him and you wonder if He is still around or if He even cares anymore.

You start convicting yourself for questioning the things that appear around you. Bitterness starts to set in, along with anger, frustration, and that loneliness that exacerbates depression. A dark spirit of your own private pain takes over your emotions. You clinch your teeth, and you attempt to avoid the obvious. You "grin and bear it." How long can you sustain that? How long can you rest assured when everything seems so bleak? You glean hope for as long as possible off of your past experiences; you realize that although it may seem dark, the light is sure to shine upon you once again. You recall the story of Job and how he lost everything, but never cursed God and God rewarded him with double all that he had lost. You pray for that same spirit that contained Job to control you.

You press on, knowing the kind of God you serve, and you thank and praise Him despite your situation. The challenges and struggles you feel are no longer your problems. You look at them and tell them they are not your concerns. You breathe and you breathe and you let go of all the tension inside of you and you relive happier times in your life.

You think back to the roof of the car when things were simple, but you focus on the great things that are standing right next to you each morning holding your hand, caring for you, and telling you that things will look up. You dream about the days you had so much to do and think about those slow days I had in Africa and you appreciate the moment.

You appreciate the subtle things that surround you. You understand that as you are fighting for a job, many are wishing they could find a way out of their jobs. You become thankful for the peace that surrounds you and for the ability to be free and not controlled by a clock or the demands of others.

Reality sets in and you see that the more you question your own faith, God has you covered. You start to see how strong your faith really is as the bills get paid, food is on the table, and small miracles and blessings come your way.

You enjoy life and take in the things that you had forgotten or taken advantage of in the past. It goes back to one of the most important things that God wants us to do: "Prepare for and go to work." As you think about work for God, the heaviness of the things that normally would bother you subside. Now you can truly have peace knowing that God has work for you and it's not your job to figure it out. It's your job to utilize your talents. It's up to you to go into the place of solitude and fast and pray so that God can speak to you and show you the weakness in you.

The weakness in you is not your lack of work; it's your lack of understanding the work God has designed for you. It's the knowledge that you do have the wisdom to come out of this situation. The weakness is in not allowing yourself to own up to how strong your faith in God really is. It's in not realizing the many talents and gifts God has given you.

Many times, we get caught up in the small stuff. We allow our circumstance to make our future or determine our destiny. Sometimes we run so fast from our circumstance that we don't realize that if we had waited a while in the pain, God would have surely brought us out to the place that He designed for us.

Faith in the War

So many times we get off the road--we hit road blocks and bumps in our drive for success. Due to our immaturity in our faith or inability to accept the cards placed in front of us, we fold. We run away from God's plan.

Think about how many people you have run out on when things didn't go completely as planned. God showed me that I have always known how to make plans, but I rarely was able to see them through. He showed me how so many times I ran out on the plan when it seemed to not be going according to my agenda. If the plan was not suitable for my lifestyle, I moved to a new plan.

I noticed that all along I should have been following his plan and seeking his direction. However, I was not prepared and did not plan accordingly to his word.

I had to learn that not having "work" was one situation that I could not run from, that I had to endure. There were many times I was able to leave my plans behind or move on to the next adventure. At that moment, God gave me a glimpse of my life and he showed me all the challenges and hard times that I ran out on due to the fact that it was not what I wanted. God not only showed me this, but he also showed me all the people that I had left standing with their hands up and lost.

It was hard to own up to possibly being the reason that some other person may have failed. However, I had to take accountability for my actions and realize that because I chose not to stay and wait it out, I may have caused another person to endure longer in the pain. After I soaked up this thought, I began to forgive myself and those who ran out on me as well; those who'd left me behind and hindered my so-called plans.

Those plans that we go after and let go of is the place that God will meet us. In spite of the situation, he will meet us even in the midst of our discontentment. It's hard to rationalize why we don't stay, but we understand clearer in our running that we only have one place to run. The place of shelter and refuge, this place is in our spirits; it is what defines us. The place I run to is my faith. We all have a place in ourselves that we hide. We all have a God that we follow and a Lord that we run to; it just may not be obvious to us who it is or where he/she is taking us. However, we all follow something--for the good or bad.

It's easy to follow the wrong plan and even easier to give up. We can soak in our misery and blame others while being consumed with anger when life throws us curve balls or takes from us. However, we must not be conformed to the situations around us.

We must learn to move around the situations and learn how to work in the place of faith and understanding. As we grow and mature, we start to realize that the things we thought were important are not; they are trivial. You really understand this when you are placed in a situation that tests your faith in people.

I envy our soldiers and the faith that they put into our government and their fellow soldiers. I wonder how a man can put so much faith into another man's hands. However, it's so difficult for us to put our faith into the hands of God.

It's amazing how strong a soldier's mind must be. The preparation it takes to discipline yourself to be ready to lose your life in a battle for something that we call "freedom." The thought of taking on an enemy force and knowing that you may never see it coming. It appeals to me and arouses my self-consciousness, making me more aware of the battle that we are all in each day: the spiritual war that we can't see.

I think, if a soldier can trust this much in a man to protect him, a man that can and has turned on him and can use his power against him, why can't I put that much more faith in God, who is much more powerful and has never turned on me but always chooses to protect me.

Each day that our soldiers go into battle, they must be fully armed and trust in the abilities of the military and its weapons. We, too, must fully put on our armor and trust in God's ability to share with us our talents, expose our own weakness, and show us how to be a part of the work he has aligned for each and every one of us.

When you have been exposed to your own weakness and you understand what makes you vulnerable, you become more aware of your environment and the people you choose to associate with. You start to rely on yourself and focus on relationships with people that can add to your strength. You make better decisions for your life and you play the role that God has ordained for you to play in the lives of those around you.

It's easy to get caught up in the battle, but how do you win the war? You don't win by staying, running, or by bringing negative people into your environment and making bad choices. You win through faith, the positive energy of those you trust in your life, and through making good decisions.

The faith that brought you to it will surely bring you out. I get that concept now. I understand why the military and so many organizations tear you down in order to build you up. It is when we are torn down that we find what we are truly capable of handling. It is in that torn position that we realize how much we need faith and how much strength the spirit will bring you.

When a person lacks faith, they lack direction. Sometimes we think we have it all figured out. We assume we know what's best for us. True faith is realizing that you don't know what's best for you; it understands that you can't make the decisions in your life necessary to win this war. You have to have faith in something outside of yourself in order to succeed and see yourself in the place you want to be.

For me, it was an awakening to know that I had faith, but limited faith. I had a faith that put a box around my circumstances. I made plans and drafted proposals, but I didn't go to the place of my faith to find out if this was the plan or the drafts that were designed for me.

It seems simple, yet so many of us do it on a regular basis. We make our own destinies--so we think. We draft the plan, we position ourselves in the right places, and we take the test. We go through all the motions of preparing for work, but in actuality it's just a job.

I'm not saying that we should not plan, prepare, and continue to go to our jobs. What I'm saying is that we need to equip ourselves and our children so that we can truly work the will that God has placed in us through our faith. We must prepare better for our work. The question becomes how do we do this?

We do this in many ways. First, we let go. We let go of our own control. We devise plans, but we always know that this plan may be changed through the will of God. We take the proper precautions, but we don't allow the outcome of these plans to be the final analysis. Life happens and it happens sometimes so fast that we don't take the time to sit back and think about what is truly important. We don't take the time to send that card of encouragement. We don't take the time, as they say, to "smell the roses" or, as I say, "slow roast the coffee."

When coffee is slowly roasted, you watch each bean as it turns and drips out into the cup of fulfillment. We are all like coffee beans; we are being refined and roasted daily. The roasting is a process that takes time but, when complete, it can be bittersweet.

The Bittersweet Smell of Coffee

I spoke about us as though we were coffee beans in the last chapter. I use this analogy not because I'm some coffee bean expert, but because I have seen the roasting process of the beans and I have smelled the bittersweet smell of the coffee: the end result.

When I studied in Tanzania and Kenya, Dr. Arens, my anthropology professor, would talk a lot about coffee. He loved coffee and was able to find common ground and connect with his students over a cup of java.

Many mornings he would venture out and bring us a cup of coffee to our rooms.

I can still smell the sweet aroma of the coffee and picture so vividly the dark hues and steam arising from the cup. As he walked into our tent, I'd see the steam fogging up his glasses, and he would enter and say, "Karibi," meaning "welcome" in Swahili.

He welcomed us each morning with open arms and knowledge to share, just as God welcomes us each morning with a new cup of life and His word to gain knowledge of His plans for us.

We were all so young, eager, and ready to learn whatever Dr. Arens could teach us about the people of the region. I pray that God makes me over each day to be like the young girl that I was in Tanzania--eager and ready to learn from His Holy Word.

The coffee was symbolic of the process we went through as students in Tanzania. It was difficult at times. He would gather us and talk about the work of the people mending the coffee bean fields and how coffee was such an important part of the morning for the people of Tanzania.

He expressed to us how it was good to find familiar grounds in order to relate to the people of the country. It was interesting to me how that cup of coffee was so symbolic of so much that went on in this life changing experience in a foreign country.

I bring up this story only because my professor was not a believer in much when it came to a God or faith. He would question me often about my strong faith. He even seemed a little moved at times when I spoke so surely about the God I served. I remember one incident when I first arrived at the school in New York as a new student and he greeted me. He was very concerned about the arrival of my passport, since I had just recently been accepted into the program and applied for one. He worried that my passport would not arrive in time for me to board with him and the rest of the students.

I assured him that I had faith that God would deliver, and he jokingly laughed at me and said, "That's great. However, I think you may need to go into Manhattan tomorrow and get you a new one. We don't want to risk you not being on our flight."

I agreed to do so, although a quiet voice in my head kept telling me, "Have faith, it will come." Even with the thoughts, I went ahead with another student into Manhattan to purchase a passport. When we were right outside the building, I placed my hand on the door to go in, but something inside my spirit told me, "No." I listened to my spirit and trusted my faith. I let go of the door and told my classmate that I would trust in my faith and not purchase the passport. She thought that I was crazy to take such a risk, but to me it was not a risk--it was merely practicing what I had been taught for so many years from watching my God work things out on my behalf.

When I returned to campus Dr. Arens greeted me and asked if I had purchased the passport. Before I could get the words off my tongue and out of my mouth, the school's librarian and another member from the study abroad team came running up to me screaming, "It came, it came! God answered your prayer." I smiled and said I knew it would come because I have faith in an awesome God. My professor raised his eyebrow and had to agree that I must serve a God that truly loves me and that I had great faith.

I tell this story only to remind myself and others that we serve a God that is conscious of all of our desires, wants, and needs. From the biggest issue to the smallest problem, God always delivers when you have faith. I know that sometimes as I'm going through in this journey of work. This story gives me such peace and joy to realize that I serve a God that never fails. He always finds ways to show up and let it be known that he is real and still in the process of developing and honoring his people. He is slowly roasting the coffee.

While reading the passport story in my journal, I also committed to memory my strong faith. I still felt encouraged, yet—I was discouraged, and I wondered where did my faith go? I asked myself do I still have the same faith at thirty–four that I had at twenty? I didn't know. I sometimes hoped that I did, but faith is a funny thing, and life has a way of testing the person with the greatest faith. Life challenges, plans going astray, folks letting you down, and just the mere factor of living can cause your faith to disintegrate into oblivion.

That's why I had to come to the paper and write this all out, not just for myself, but for others who may be experiencing the same state of affairs or a similar condition. I know that someone out there is going through what I'm going through, especially with not being able to find work. It's astonishing to me the number of people out of work, discouraged, hopeless, and losing faith. I started to become one of these people, until that day I saw the sermon about going to work.

I was liberated by those words. It fully put things into perspective. Don't get me wrong, I still have days that I feel down and distraught. However, I'm thankful for the jobs that God has given me. I know that on many of those jobs I was able to work, and when my work was complete, God moved me from that situation.

I still must remind myself about the faith that I had as a teenager and how that faith led me to many places in life where I'm sure God used me to work. I know he used me to work on my professor and many of the students and people in Tanzania and Kenya.

It's really no coincidence, in my mind, that out of seventeen students on a trip to a foreign country, I was brought to be in the company of atheists, non-believers, Muslims, Jews, and other religions of the world that I was not familiar with. Being from such a small, conservative Catholic family from the Midwest, it was wonderful to be able to speak often about my faith and to experience so many small and large miracles right before my eyes.

It is this hope that I had and the faith I depended on in Tanzania that I find myself going to these days for reassurance. I know that God gives us many experiences to comfort us when we are being tested.

Dreams and Vision

Today my test is all based around a misfortune that took place in my life. The prayer is still the same, and the faith is the place it begins for me. I know that eventually He will show me His will and His desire, and I will be given the work He has planned for me.

At this time, I only can accept the fate of my life and the decisions I make and pray that I please God and that, in my suffering, I'm able to continue to see the good and limitless possibilities of this world. I have always had the mindset that you first have a dream, then a vision, and it forms into reality.

I wrote an entire paper on this concept when I was just fifteen, and I still remember many of the words from that paper. I recall the times that I would dream, and then I would start to envision the dream, and eventually it would come to pass.

It's funny how when we are young and full of hope and faith, we can dream so big and our visions are so clear. I never thought I'd find myself visionless. However, as I stated before, it's muddy these days and I can't seem to make it clear. It's no secret that the cruel ways of this world can start to erode the human spirit--if you allow it.

I think that's when your faith truly is brought into play, because I realize as a child you need to have those dreams and visions come together fast and quick and work out in your behalf in order to build faith. As you get older, your faith becomes more of a challenge, based on the outcomes. Things don't happen as fast; God seems to take His time. He works our patience and tests us to see how loyal we are and how true we are to His purpose for our lives.

He has worked my faith; He has challenged many of my dreams and made unclear my visions. However, I still find ways to encourage myself through the pain. I know that his voice leads me; it whispers softly to me, "Peace, and be at ease for I have you."

I feel my skin crawl and my eyes water as I draw nearer to Him. I find myself torn in this world of havoc as it collides with the world that I dreamed of as a child. I run into my own mind, and I gather stories of my past and present. I capture the essence of all the great miracles He has brought me through. I think of situations He has brought my family through. I recall the day when

34

I was five and was hit by a car, and how the impact knocked me out cold. I remember feeling the warmth of love surrounding me. I remember Him whispering to me to have faith, and through my faith He would complete me and put me to work.

I never understood what that meant or why that car hit me that day, and why I always felt so connected to my faith after that incident. However, today as I sit and write these words, The Lord has shown me His favor. Because of His favor, I'm able to have faith and share the moments that He has delivered me. Although I may appear to be in a dark moment of my life, because of situations such as the car incident, I know I serve a God that has work for me.

Instead of contemplating what should be and how I like it to be, I bless him for what he has done already for me. So many times we sing songs that say, "Lord, if you did nothing else for me, I still praise you." However, I wonder how true that really is for many of us. I even question my own faith with these words. I have to remind myself that He has done enough already, and that He will continue to always do exceedingly and abundantly more than I could ever ask or hope for, even as doors close in my face. I know that He will provide.

These words transform me into who I am and who I will become. We all speak of transforming and being prepared. But how do we transform without pain? How do we exceed who we ever thought we could be without finding ways to encourage ourselves in times of drought and despair? We lean into our past hopes and fears and we gather strength from overcoming these times in our lives. We celebrate the small victories that take place, and we move forward in a new and transformed spirit of faith.

The Plan

The months went by and I still found myself without work. I found myself having a harder time seizing on to my faith. I found myself handcuffed and chained to the bondage of my circumstances. It started to overshadow all the small victories in my life. I began to speculate on the outcome of each interview, and I started to realize that I was being transformed in my faith.

My faith was taking me to a new level of expectation, and I didn't want to think that I had been abandoned by His will. Nevertheless, I started to question my faith and ponder what happened to my "job, not work" mindset. I started to relinquish the thought of going to work. and I started to focus once again on finding a job. I knew that I had to have faith, and I believed that God knew best, but it became arduous waiting on the right work to come my way.

I gathered my feelings and started to fast and pray. I deactivated my Facebook account and silenced my phone, only answering calls intermittently. I found myself very frayed by the entire situation. I became unmotivated and disheartened by my inability to focus on my plan; a plan that I drafted and re-drafted and drafted again. It became ambiguous where my faith stood.

I started to call out to God and ask Him to renew my heart and mind, to help me devise the plan He wants for me. I thought I had found the answers, and I assumed I knew my role. However, in my quest to find a job versus going to work, in some way I got off task and ventured into a hustle for a job. I allowed the outside situation of losing my unemployment to discourage my faith and transform me back into the thinking of my past.

I started to search hastily for a job, although God had already told me that I needed to prepare for work. I ignored my spirit and went with my instincts and my emotions and started to plunge into the field of finding a job. I listened to the skeptics around me that had no clue what it was like to be out of work for over 16 months and go on numerous job interviews with thousands of applicants only to be told that they would keep my resume on file.

It became a joke, a school market of places to post for work on an anonymous black board. Your resume would go off into this night ride, and you would not know if an actual person even ever looked at your credentials.

It became even more apparent that others were having the same difficulties. I started to listen to the mummers and complainers and became one myself. I had to regroup, refocus, and evaluate what God had shared with me in Pastor Bryant's sermon. However, even that sounded like a hoax to me after a while.

My faith was definitely being transformed. It was being transformed and lost. I tried to recapture things of my past to draw from, and I only would become bitter at the situation that took place. I started to do something that I said I never would do and that was become an "I could of, should of, wish I" person.

I started to have regret. Regret was something I had never had in my life, but emotions are overwhelming when you are a person who followed all the rules and did everything by the book, and it didn't work. I found myself not reaping from following all the rules, and this caused me to question my faith.

I would watch the news and see so much corruption, lies, and abuse taking place in my city. These incidents would really test my faith. I would remember back to how these same shenanigans caused me to lose my job. I tried hard not to focus on the negative, but it appeared that all around me in the world all I could see and find was negative.

It became very overpowering, and I recalled a time when I had chosen to turn off and get rid of my television. I wanted to lock myself in a room and never come out. I didn't know how to cope with the misfortunes around me and all the things I was experiencing while searching for work. I went to so many interviews and was not impressed with much of the follow up or the interview process.

I kept telling myself that I never wanted to go back into an environment that felt heavy and produced such a stressful atmosphere as the one I had left. When I would recall all the lies being told and the manipulation taking place at my former employer's office, I would start to re-evaluate my faith, yet again, and cry.

I started to come back to reality and realized the favor God had shown me on that job in spite of a few bad seeds. God had blessed me and protected me with a few good seeds. I was grateful for those who really had come to my side and tried to defend me or help me in my role at my prior company. I started to think about the pressure everyone was under and how we were there to help others yet couldn't find the same help that we so amiably gave out within our own organization.

My fears arose in me and took me back to the day that my manager came to me with so much nonsense and tried to use her power and position to control me. I was so shocked that a manger would come with such foolishness and expect me to be okay with it. I remembered going to Human Resources on several occasions just to get away from her tomfoolery, but to no avail. I recalled how I knew I had to have faith that the truth would come out and set me free.

I remembered that my path was greater than my situation and that although I had a long tough road to venture, I had a great God that loved me. It was then that my faith began to transform again. My faith went from what I could see, to the hope of what I wanted to see, to the ability to just be able to have faith again. It transformed my understanding that faith in people will lead you astray every time, and it reconfirmed to me that my faith in self and God was all I needed.

Forgiveness
and Healing

After realizing my faith was being tested and starting to see it transformed, I went through a period of forgiveness. I always was a person that easily forgave; I can recall forgiving so many wrongs that were done to me. The first time I ever truly remember having to forgive was in first grade when I was chosen to be the song leader for mass at my small Catholic School in Indiana.

My teacher decided at the last minute to allow two other girls from class to be the song leader based on a promise she had made to them when they had been over her house the week prior. I remember being so upset and hurt. I somehow got past it with the help of my parents, and I forgave her. Shortly thereafter she came to me and apologized for the incident and the next time the first grade was in charge of mass she allowed me to be the song leader.

Looking back at that situation, I now realize how minor it was and that I had no reason to get my panties all up in a bunch. However, even at six years old, it started to change my faith in people. It prepared me for the many setbacks I would receive in my life due to others not being able to be trusted. I think of how blessed I was to come from a home with two wonderful parents and learn from them how to forgive and trust. I can rarely recall having to forgive many people as a child, but I'm thankful for the lesson and experience I received from my first grade teacher--it truly prepared me.

It was hard for me to realize that the entire world was not as kind, loving, or supportive as the environment I had grown up in. It was difficult to have people lie to your face, deceive you, and want to deliberately harm you in some cases. This was apparent so many times in my personal life and on many of my jobs.

I know many of us have experienced going into our jobs just to work and complete a task, but negative energy from faithless people can appear and hinder our success. I know that, for me, this type of behavior caused lots of pain and set-backs in my career. This is not a healthy situation for anyone.

Given that what I had experienced many times in the past from former employers was wrong, it was very difficult for me to forgive. God is still dealing with my heart on this situation. That's why I know that God has to show us our weakness. In our weakness we meet Him and are complete. For me, the weakest state is disappointing others and having others disappoint me. It's a challenge to overcome obstacles that can breed resentment and harm so many other areas of your life.

Many times, we don't realize that we have not truly forgiven a person, situation, or a thing. When I was younger, it seemed so simple to forgive and move forward.

In my adult years, there were people that I thought I had forgiven. Yet fifteen years later, even an apology from former friends and boyfriends can still hurt like the event had just taken place. You learn to move past it, and you forgive in spite of the emotions and scars that sometimes stay in your heart for years.

It's these scars and wounds that others leave you that allow you to be open for God's healing process. In His healing you find out your weakness and you're able to confront your past and present as you reconnect your faith to your future.

All of these pains, rejections, disappointments, and hurts accumulate into a total healing package. The healing package is the real meaning behind your faith. Your faith grows in your healing. It took me a while to understand that faith and adversity go hand in hand. I know that, like me, many of you have come to recognize the value of your faith more during these tribulations and calamities of life.

For me, it's been a true healing process that some may understand and others may ridicule. Unless you have been in a situation that comes up against the core of your being, you have no idea. I was placed in a situation based on someone's biased judgments and lies, and I felt defeated. Situations like this really test your faith in mankind. It becomes a reflection of your faith in yourself and in God.

You recall that God made man in his image and through this recognition your spirit struggles with this connection. The knowledge that a man could hinder your life in such a horrific matter, yet he is a reflection of the God you love and serve. There is something about this revelation that draws a wedge in your faith. Then you realize that God chose to put you in the situation in order for you to overcome your weakness and unite with Him in your faith.

This was overwhelming for me. It was a trial of my soul; it tortured my spirit and I battled with it in my flesh. I tried to find ways to walk in peace in the knowledge that God was preparing me for His work. I had to realize that this was not the end of the road. I told myself over and over again that this was a test of my faith to show how I was able to overcome my weakness, my fears, my inhibitions, and all that encompasses me. I knew that through writing and walking in these words I would transform my faith.

My faith was transformed through my willingness to forgive those who hurt me in the past and that will hurt me in the future. I knew that through this journey I would discover my work. I knew that I would not discover my work until I had completed this journey of faith being restored through learning how to truly forgive.

It's amazing how God creates balance not only in the natural world but also in the spirit. The key to finding these small victories and joys in life involves being ready to open yourself up to your own weaknesses. We blind ourselves when we believe that we forgive so easily or that we have such great hearts that only desire good. We need to be able to except the evil in ourselves that does not always desire good. When we find the balance between our own weakness and greatness, we find the ability to connect with God. We understand more fully our heart and we are more willing to give it over to God.

We are not always as forgiving as we think. I came to realize this for myself when a situation from my past came back to haunt me, and I felt the pain hit me like the day it first occurred. The emotion was strong; it might have even been stronger today than it was at that time. The hate, the hurt, and the betrayal, it all led to me having an unforgiving heart.

Although it had been years since I had even dealt with the situation, it was rewarding to know that I still was human and had much work to do. I still had pain and much growth in my faith and forgiveness.

Today, I can say that I'm still healing from the many circumstances that have occurred throughout my life that have caused me to build up anger or resentment. But this is only a process. A process that we must all go through alone, a process that is needed for many to come to that place of work in which God would and will lead you. It starts with the choices we make in the heart. It's our choice to relinquish the animosity, not hold onto our fears, and learn to forgive.

God showed me that I like to run. I think about one particular incident as a teenager that God allowed me to suffer and, although it may have been way over my maturity level, instead of forgiving, I just ran. I thought that I had forgiven and left, but I never forgave. I held onto bitterness and hate and ran.

I think about this and many other moments in my life that came to me and I didn't forgive. There are times in our lives that situations come across our paths when things outside of us are bigger than we can handle, or so we think. In these situations, we learn not to trust, and we lose faith. Instead of waiting on and seeking God in the situation, we run and make more unforgiving situations for ourselves.

All in all, I know that God will always direct my path and that He ultimately will be the one who controls my destiny. I know that my destiny is greatly connected to my past because without acknowledging, accepting, and forgiving the things in our past, we can't fully be prepared for our future. Our future (yours and mine) involves connecting our forgiveness of the past to our faith of the present and future. Our faith is beyond what we see in the present or have experienced in our past. Faith is based on a timeless energy, a source that reconnects us to our hopes and establishes our destiny. Without first finding forgiveness, we can't move forward in faith which leads to us prospering in our future.

Embracing Weakness

I realized that many of my issues continue to follow me into my future. I have not united my past forgiveness with my present faith. I have declined to unite them willingly. I was too consumed with my present condition. I was unaware that my present circumstance was a direct reflection of my past resentments and my inability to face my future challenges.

We all have those past places, people, and things that we must move forward from. We carry these things over to our present and they hinder our faith. We must learn to forgive and truly let go. Instead of running from prior conditions, we must stand firm and unite with our past concerns and allow our present faith to intervene for us.

When we channel all the negative energy out and re-sort to filling up on the positive of what our future holds for us, we move closer into walking in our works.

This has been a challenge. A challenge that prior to being put into my current unemployed situation, I was totally disengaged from and unaware that it was even a problem. I had no clue that so much was still holding me down and keeping me in bondage. I'm so much about being free and not controlled that I had failed to realize I was still under the control of my past pain.

It is pain that we all will be faced with at some point in our lives in some capacity, whether it's death, divorce, separation, loss of a job, or just the consequences of sin. We all experience some form of being disconnected from the freedom we all love, enjoy and, would like more of by not doing the works that God has created for us.

In order for us to get to work for God, we have to take on the quality at His core and that is LOVE. We must embrace the love that God represents in His word. In order for us to go to work for Him, love is essential. We think that we are living God's will or working for God, yet we don't share the love that He requires in His word of us.

Love is not just an emotion or a word. It's a condition that's required of us in order to fulfill his works. After listening to Pastor Bryant's sermon, I contemplated how I get to work. I meditated on these words for many months, and God showed me that I must find and learn to embrace His love and He would enable me to work.

He revealed to me that his greatest commandment is the key for us to get to work: "Love thy neighbors, as much as you love thyself." This is a commandment given to us directly from Jesus in the scripture. We have to find the place of love within that allows us to show it to His people. We dwell in the value of love where forgiveness is not an option, it's a must.

There are many places that have taken me to the place of jubilation, the place that I find myself tied up in the moment, and everything around me goes silent. It's a feeling that I get when I write, or when I'm acting. This feeling engulfs me to the point where nothing around me matters because I'm caught up in the love of my craft that God has given me. I must find that same love for His people. We all must find that love in order to get to work.

In order to move forward in His love, we have to become those words for ourselves. We must embrace the good, the bad, and the ugly and recognize our own faults. We have to be exposed to our weakness and find ways to love ourselves despite our short comings. People can feel that they have self-love, but if they truly look within and compare their love for self with the word of God, they will see that they don't truly love themselves.

In order to embrace love for yourself, you must first dare to connect faith with forgiveness. Once you have connected your faith to forgiveness, you can start to see your weakness, embrace your imperfections, and start the process of learning how to love yourself and see yourself as God sees you.

When we learn to take on our own infirmity, we learn to love like God loves, although we must realize we will never have the perfect love to show another human being that God surrenders to us each day. This should be our goal and the place where we examine and compare our love. We can open our hearts of acceptance by being vulnerable enough to know that we are weak and, through this weakness, strive to love like God.

In our weakness, God meets us and he pours his blessings upon us. He opens our hearts to receive the promises He vows to us in His word, that He will give us the desires of our hearts. He does this as we unite our broken, misguided, lonely, and confused hearts with His heart of love. When you become susceptible to see your unclean heart's desires, you realize that they only can lead you to a job.

However, God's call is bigger for each and every one of us. He calls for us to emulate His love even when we are in pain. The pain of our past will meet with the faith of our present situation and allow us to work towards that completion in Him as He delivers us into our future work.

This had to be one of the hardest places for me to dwell. In my pain, I had a difficult time accepting God's love. I was unable to hold onto His word many nights. It was in my pain that bitterness, anger, and hate would start to grow. I had to re-examine my mind and realign my emotions to His word. I forced myself to make different choices. I had to learn how to center my soul on His spirit and gain strength in my flesh to continue to love and walk in faith.

As we move forward in love, we understand that we are not a separate being outside of Him, but we complete Him as much as He completes us. He has given us many components of himself so that we don't feel incomplete or as if we are failures. There is no failure in His love. That's why it's so important that we remain aware of our weakness and we remain aware of His love.

Through His love, He imports in us the fundamentals of life. Due to sin, we will never be absent of pain or misfortunes, but we can choose how we deal with these difficulties of life through how we love in spite of our own situations. We make the choices for our life. It is in our hour of pain that we are brought to the perfection of God's Grace.

As we allow ourselves to move forward in love, we find ways to connect to our work. Pastor Bryant's words, for me, were deeper than just finding a job as a means to live or as a place to go in order to make money. I trust that we all realize that we must find a job in order to survive in this world. However, my hope, and what I believe to be Pastor Bryant's point, is that we start to prepare and ask God to put us to work versus going to and asking Him to give us a job.

Hunger and Hopelessness

I know many of us who feel that we are just working at a job, but that is not true. What God revealed to me is that we are all going to work in some form or fashion; we just have to be aware of who we are working for and with. The work we do is not as important as having the wisdom to realize the work was sent by God.

I know I need a job, and I'm completely aware of my circumstances. I can't afford to be choosy when it comes to picking my work. It's been a battle to find gainful and meaningful employment these past months. I'm aware of my needs. I'm more aware, in fact I'm consciously aware, that God has a plan. He has an agenda for my life, although many times His plan for my life is not exactly in line with what I think my life should look like. I know that ultimately His will is a far better choice for my life than my desires or expectations.

When you learn to let go of your expectations and embrace God's work you are able to connect to your faith and develop a deeper relationship with yourself and God. This journey that I have been on and continue on is a tough road; it's had triumphs, disappointments, and setbacks. However, I can't rest and wallow in the mishaps of my circumstance. I can't sit back defeated, complaining, and crying everyday about my unfair circumstances. I have to realize that God made a decision to put me in this place for a reason.

I have no clue what all this means or why it occurred to me. I do know that I'm blessed, I'm highly favored, and I have many talents and skills to offer this world. I can't allow the few wrongs of many to influence the rest of my life.

I have to come to a place of forgiveness and move forward in love and try to find a way to connect to the work that God would have me connected to. The longer I sit around complaining, crying, and upset about what has happened to me, the worse my chances of success become.

I know that I'm not the only one going through what I'm dealing with. I want to share my testimony. I want you to realize it's a process that we all have to find our way through.

However, in this process we must learn that God is able; we must think on the positive and channel our energy into asking for and looking for work. We must speak into ourselves what the word declares for us. We can't allow our outward circumstances to become our permanent dwelling. I have to remind myself every day that God does have work for me. He has opportunities, and He is aligning every piece of this puzzle called my life.

I told myself that, no matter what, I will continue to hold my head high. I will continue to fight against wrongs when they do occur, but I will depend on my wisdom when it comes to finding work. It can be discouraging, trust me. I've applied to numerous companies, sat through several interviews, written presentations and papers, and still have failed to come up with a job.

My eyes are swollen shut from all the tears brought on by closed doors. There are many people who don't understand and will never relate to being in a position that you can't change on your own. I hear and read the comments of those who feel when you are unemployed it's somehow your fault when you don't obtain work. I hear many of them even say that you just don't want to work. I can say, for me and many others out there in my unemployed position, this is just not true.

These negative people will never understand your hunger to work. How the taste is so real in your mouth and the craving in your stomach is almost unbearable. How the hunger pains creep up on you in the late night, but you have no food to calm the raging war in your gut. They are not there when you sit in your bed at night and your mind is tormented by the lack of opportunities to come your way. They don't see the thoughts on your mind as you sleep and dream about the interview you had that day. How the company that interviewed you praised your performance and led you to believe that the job was yours. You just know this is the one. Only, in the morning, you are disappointed once again and told that they went with another candidate over you.

It takes you back to your memories of high school as you're searching for love and appear to have found "the one." You are led to believe there is no one else better for you, only to find out that this is not the case. You don't understand how the two of you danced the night away so gracefully and everything seemed to be on one accord. Until later that evening or the next morning you find out that they had not only danced the night away with you, but several others. This search for work is a dance that many nights you are dancing alone. It becomes draining and can be daunting. It feels as if you will never find that perfect fit.

However, like love, you don't want to give up on your pursuit. So you continue to find partners to dance with and you dance, and sometimes the dance appears to go perfect and other times you stand on the wall and watch as others dance. However, you stay in the moment and you enjoy each chance to court a new opportunity.

Trust me I've been in it, and I'm going through it as I write these words. No one can give you words to satisfy the discontentment you have within as you search relentlessly for work. You begin to relate these experiences to past experiences that formed you into the person you are today.

It was these experiences that, at the time, were the thorns in your side. This experience of not finding work becomes your new thorn, and you lose hope as your faith evaporates into thin air. Your stomach tangles in knots, and you feel all alone in this battle. You watch as all your friends become employed, hoping and wishing that you are next. However, just as in love, you doubt that the opportunities are out there, and when you do land that interview, as in times before, you have to overcome the pessimistic voices in your head. You have to encourage and uplift yourself--no matter the outcome.

This self-motivation takes and adds to your character. Each day forward all you can do is look back at your past experiences and try to draw out of it what God would have you gain. You remind yourself of His favor and love.

I have come to realize that work does not define who I am as a person. But I, just like you, add to the work my own unique and special talents that only I can give to an organization or company.

This is the hardest part. As I stated in the beginning, it's great knowing that God has work for you not a job-- but knowing is only half the battle. How do you survive, how do you stay sane, how do you keep from losing your mind?

These are questions we all ponder; ones we all come up against when we are in drastic situations or going through the process of finding out that our plans have been changed. You think about the "how," "when," and "why" and you focus in on the things out of your reach. If you have children, your only thought is to protect and care for them; you try to find ways to make their sufferings less. It can all be quite overwhelming when you wake up and realize the plans that you had have been changed. That the course you were on is no longer an option. What is a person to do when everything they know to live for, have fought for, sacrificed, or have been taught is stripped from them in an instant? Your whole way of life is no longer in existence. The system you had grown to accept and utilize no longer wants you and has eradicated you from its plan.

How do you cope in your pain? How do you overcome your confusion? How do you go out and continue to battle on a field that seems to not want to protect you? What do you do? For me, I heard a calling. I heard a sermon, and those words stuck with me and continue to be my source of inspiration.

I understood in my private pain that God has His own plan and that He never intended for me to just take a job. He wants me to work His will to see His people to the place of love that He has stored up for them. He wants to open up pathways to His rivers and flow them upon His people as they turn their hearts to forgive, so that He can cleanse their hearts and move them into the place of work.

Lemons

into Lemonade

I will admit, I still cry and I do not claim to know the next move for me. I try to dream, but it's blank. I try to have a vision, and it's unclear. However, as I see a glimpse of hope on my muddy window, I look up. I look up, and I realize that these are not my concerns. I understand that to get to where I need to be, I must truly let go and let God move in me what He sees fit to move for me. I understand that I must think and see the positive of all situations and find love even in the hate that surrounds me.

I must go after what He aligns my heart to desire, and as I plan and write proposals I can't always be the one in control of the pen. Destiny is not in my hands; it's not my choice to make for me. It's not in my control. What's in my control is my outlook, my thoughts, my acknowledgement, and my finding a way to get past the pain to be able to see the work that is out there to be done.

I don't know why God inspired me to write these pages--it was just heavy on my heart. I don't know how many people will be encouraged or even understand the magnitude of the situation at hand. What I do know is that we all struggle, we all go through pain, and we all have bumps in the road. However, we must never lose faith.

We must always search within ourselves to see past the muddy windows. We are not in this alone, and it will never be completely understood. I don't know if work will ever find me or vice versa. What I know is that I've been out of work for 16 months, I lost my job over nonsense, and now I'm in a place that feels like it's all closing in on me. Yet, I still stand. I'm no longer running; I'm not allowing my mishaps to control my future. I'm looking opportunity in the eye as I say, "Here I am, and I am coming for you."

My faith may not be as strong as it was 15 years ago; it just might be weaker or perhaps even stronger. However, it's still here. My faith is the answer to all my prayers. No more muddy windows for me, not that they are now clean. I just know that the Lord has seen me and He gave me a word to give.

So, smile in hope, love, and faith, knowing that you also have work and never settle for just a job because God never intended for us to be unhappy, disappointed, misused people that go to jobs. He intended on us to work and celebrate our life and our testimony. I hope that my words can be a testimony for those ready to give up. I hope that they know that this is not a permanent situation; it's just an opportunity waiting to be seized--go to work and find the journey set up for your life.

Although we may smile in the hope and love of finding our work and connecting it to our faith, we must never stop while on this journey. My sister, Stephanie, tells me that we have to "turn our lemons into lemonade and make a profit." I watch many people on my journey of unemployment. I observed some be successful and find work and others find jobs. However, there were a few that didn't find anything and lost everything. I know some that couldn't see past the moment to carry out the journey and, in the end, the enemy won.

A few of the victims lost the battle with their changed attitudes, some became so bitter, so distraught with their circumstances, that they lost all hope and became hardened. Others became so depressed that they slept their pain away.

A few never woke from their naps because they decided that they would sleep forever. Even though I can't rationalize with all of these decisions, I understand the pain and the despair of those who became victims to their circumstance. I, too, went through my changes and had a choice to make. I could have become a victim to all of these scenarios. The only difference is that I had work that I knew God wanted me to do.

I had grace that covered me, prayers that linked me, and love that embraced me. I don't judge those who have different paths; I just want to put a word out there for those of you who may be contemplating and going through as victims. I say to you, DO NOT allow your JOURNEY to end with you as a victim. I know that

God has a plan, He has a purpose, and He wills that we all come out victorious in the end. We must not become victims to our current circumstances.

I know, for me, there were days of emptiness and I'd think to myself--is this all an illusion, is this journey worth proceeding with in faith? What shall I hold onto when I feel like everything is moving around me, and I'm still standing in the same place? When I feel as if I'm stuck under a dark cloud that's raining on me? I breathe, as I always do, and I smile. I know that as long as there is breath, there is a divine purpose for my life. I have meaning, and I have a will that needs to be carried out. I have a journey that I must take and, even though at times it may feel as though I'm alone on this path, I'm never alone in my faith. We are never alone in our faith as long as we hold onto God.

As I move each day in the path that is laid before me, I watch as others go about their day. They go to work, or shall I say to jobs. They dress up, put on their happy face, and entertain life--yet many of them are lost. They, too, are lonely on this road. They never know when the pink slip will come, and they are holding on trying to re-main in control. I know because I've been on the other side.

Now I'm finding peace on this side. I found that it's easier not to worry when you have no control of the cir-cumstance you're in. I know this may sound strange, but when you know God is in control His words become more real and you realize that His "yoke is easy." It's amusing to see how God will work each day out; I laugh as I type these words because it's funny that God has so many problems to take care of out there. His concerns are way bigger than my little journey. I'm just a little piece of this amazing puzzle. I don't even have much that I really should be worried about. Sometimes on these journeys of misfortune, we forget that this is nothing. This is just a second in the mind of God, and at any moment He can change our entire situation.

The Spiritual Battle

I watch as God works things out all around me. I know that it is only Him working things in my behalf. A few months ago, my journey was more difficult and had new challenges and obstacles to overcome.

One morning I woke up with severe pains in my knees; I could barely walk up and down stairs. My entire body hurt, and my heart felt as though it would fall out my back as the pressure of what felt like a knife stabbed me over and over again. I went to the doctor concerned about the pain in my chest and body. He noticed some changes in me, so he ordered various tests--one set happened to be for muscle diseases. Neither I nor the doctor had any clue of the outcome of these tests and had no idea what was really making me ill.

The numbers in my blood work came back a few weeks later, and they were extremely elevated. It looked as though I might have lupus--an autoimmune disease. My doctor assumed the worst and sent me to a specialist for more tests. For several weeks I laid in bed in pain.

I was scared, although I had the love and support of my family. I felt alone and found myself in a battle that only I could fight. It was at this moment in my journey that a job became so unimportant to me. I realized that a job was not worth my health or as important as my life.

I got angry at all the wasted time I had invested in so many companies that never took the time to invest back into me. Now, don't get me wrong. I have worked for some wonderful people. I have been blessed by many of the companies that I worked for in the past. Even the last employer I worked for, the one that brought me so much turmoil, led me to some wonderful people and helped me develop some valuable life skills.

However, as I lay in the bed, many negative thoughts ran through my head. I thought about how I might not live to see my children grow up; my boys were only 8 and 5 at the time. How do you tell your young children that you may not be able to run with them, you may not make it to their game, or just might not be around?

These were the thoughts the enemy placed in my head, although I should have known better than to have these thoughts since this was not my first scare in life with an illness or harmful situation. I still was scared, and fear started to take a toll on me. As I lay in fear, God came to me and through my spirit He showed me how

He had healed me so many times throughout my life and that I had no reason to fear.

He brought back to my memory the car accident at age five, my breast tumor in my early teens, the meningitis that had stricken me one summer in college in my twenties, and the staph infection that I had one year in my early thirties. I thought on all this and laughed as I realized that the enemy was up to his same little tricks. He doesn't change his game. He just comes with new diagnoses, new companies, and new people. God revealed to me that all that I was going through was an attack. It no longer was a physical attack for me; it had now become a spiritual battle for my soul.

When I got this revelation, I got out bed and I told myself that I was no longer ill and that I would not believe any report but that of the Lord. Weeks went by and my body still ached; however, things got easier and the pain started to subside. It finally came time for me to see the specialist that my family doctor had recommended. I went in, still a little scared, but I kept speaking words to myself, "God has work for me to do, and I can't do this work if I'm not healthy." I refused to take any diagnosis other than a clean bill of health.

A week went by after all the testing and then a few more weeks went by and I had no results. Fear came over me again, but peace would always reappear. Finally, I got the phone call from the doctor and I was told more tests were being run because they wanted to be sure it was not a cancer or other disease.

As I waited for my results, I was sent to a heart specialist for more tests. It became test after test, and finally the doctor called me one day, as I lay in pain in my depression, and told me everything looked good and that I definitely did not have lupus or cancer. I was relieved, although my body still was in pain. I was happy to know that God had answered my prayer and that He was still working for me. I realized that I too must start working for Him.

The journey is a long road; it can be very painful and agonizing to be in a place where you have no control. I didn't understand why God kept placing me in positions where I had no control. It appeared that for several years I was in this place. I felt like I was just there and that everything around me was taking place, but I couldn't stop it or find any answers to correct it. I had to just stay on the road and allow what I was going through to occur.

I tell the story of this journey because so many of us lose faith and hope on our own paths of discovery. I know how hard it can be when you are in a place and you have no control. You have no way of dictating the outcome. I know that many people who decide to take this crucial time to change things by taking control normally go at it the wrong way and make the wrong choices.

This is the time that many who become so beat down by the things around them decide to take matters into their own hands. I understand your feelings and your pain. I'm telling you to never take it into your own hands. Your hands will never be in control. What do you gain by trying to stop what God has planned? This is all a part of the "roasting process." It's the time that He builds you and connects your faith to your forgiveness.

This is the place where he starts to connect you to work. He takes you to the road that He wants for your life. I write this to let people know that the journey is not ours. We never were made to control our situations or outcomes in life. We were made to allow God to work through us and for us. It is when we decide to work for ourselves that we find ourselves in this place of no control.

The place of no control is where God wants us to be so that He can take our journey and make it His own. We must not fight what the plan for us will be; we have to find a way to connect to it so that we can be ready to work and make the right choices based on God's call for our life.

Control and Steam

Control--I never knew how much it had over my life until I started going through all my situations and taking this journey of unemployment. I know I laugh a lot at my situations. I always used to get in trouble in school for laughing and smiling too much. When you really think about it, why would a teacher discipline a child for laughing and smiling? I know it's off the subject, but really, what harm is a laugh or a smile going to do to the class environment? I will never understand that; even as an adult it stills blows my mind. However, it might have something to do with being in control.

We all seek control; we like to know that we have it all together. It's great to appear to others that you have control, but behind every person that appears to be controlled is a raging river, a boiling pot of water, ready to explode. I didn't realize how many people were so full of steam. I think we all have enough steam in us to never have to go and purchase a Starbuck's drink, because with our own steam we can make plenty of froth after we get done with our roasting process.

No one would ever think that they have steam in them. However, let folks lie on you long enough, ridicule you, make false accusations against you, take your job, harm your kids, or just whatever boils you up and you will see that you have plenty of steam.

This steam sometimes is not always right in our face; we may not even know that we carry some of this hot power beneath our pressed suits or in our Mark Jacob bags. However, we all do. We carry this steam. This steam is the control we all are fighting for in life. We want control of our lives and everything around it. We have been placed in a culture that thrives on control. Capitalism is a result of our desire to control. We want to control all the money, cars, houses, anything we can. We may not even realize that we value control. I didn't realize that I had this problem; however, the mere thought of me believing I didn't have this problem was part of my own control.

I realized this when all of the things that I depended on, trusted in, and worked so hard to obtain didn't pan out the way I expected. In these situations, did I start to see the ugliness of my control. It goes back to grade school. I remember when all the kids would play at the park and a few of the "bad" boys in my class wanted to try and raise the girl's skirts and run and laugh at them.

I, not wanting them to do these things to me, would pay them off in order to have control of the situation. Yep! I would give them parts of my lunch, or my entire lunch, just so they wouldn't humiliate me like they did the other girls. It worked, and I learned that I could control a lot of what happened to me in my life, or so I thought.

I thought that if I could just go through life and do all the right things, know all the right people, pay the right amount of money, make all the right decisions, and follow the right God I would have all the control. No, I'm just kidding, I didn't think that, at least not consciously. However, I lived that way and many of us live this way without even realizing we do. We are so caught up in trying to control, dictate, manipulate, and make all the situations around us work for us. We are a product of our society, of our political powers, and of a capitalist nation.

I think it sometimes is an unconscious thing that we as human beings do without ever knowing what we are doing to ourselves or the people around us. I never felt like I was a control freak or that I manipulated situations to go in my favor. I just did what I saw and lived what I thought was a "right" life. He showed me that there had been times in my life that I lived as though I was in control. During those times, my life was the most screwed up.

He showed me that the only control I had was to give my control up to either Him or the things that surrounded me. So, for years, I gave my control to the things that surrounded me. I gave my control to my parents as a child (in most cases they do know what's best). As a pre-teen, I gave that control to my friends and peers, and as a teenager it was given to my boyfriend. In my early adulthood, I gave the control to my religion and my jobs. Finally, in my mature adult years and current situation, that control was handed over to my husband, my kids, and to my unemployed circumstance.

We probably don't even realize that we surrender so much to the people, circumstances, and things around us, and all along, God is standing there waiting for us to surrender our control to him. I had a hard time writing this because it is difficult to realize where your control truly lies in your life.

We all must face the music. We all have to realize, understand, and come to grips with whom and what is controlling our lives. I'm sure that, just as I was able to uncover where my control was being surrendered, many of you will be able to uncover who and what is controlling your life.

That's what my unpleasant situation did for me and what yours will do for you; it will have you searching yourself, examining your thoughts, your life, your passions, your mistakes, and uncovering where you need to be and how you can get there. I asked God to forgive me for allowing others and things to control me throughout my life. I also asked God to forgive me for controlling myself (so I thought) and asked Him to control me and to help me lose myself and become more out of control for him.

To many people, this sounds ludicrous to say that you want to become more out of control. However, for me it was exactly where I needed to be. I needed to be so out of control that I had no choice but to surrender totally to God. It's in those times of being out of control that we can allow His spirit to take control of you. This became my liberating moment.

So many folks don't know how to let go and allow themselves to be out of control and to face the reality that they know nothing at all and that everything that they have been and are doing at this present moment are all wrong. They have been the ones in control, which we all know means that they are giving their control to something or someone. When we lose control and allow God to be that force that fills us with His spirit, we don't care how things appear in the natural world.

I guess this is the place that David went to in the scripture when he danced out of his clothes. His wife was there and watched and became ashamed and embarrassed because of his actions. I think that's most of our problems too. We don't want to be embarrassed; we don't want to look different or be labeled weird.

I got over that a long time ago. Now I'm able to be out of control, and I have freed myself from all the restrictions that others place upon us and we place on ourselves. I have allowed myself not to depend on the things that I see but to gain the faith to trust in what I do not see. I'm not restricting myself anymore.

One restriction for me was my job. Yes! My job was a restriction that controlled me. I was controlled by the clock, by the folks that I had to answer to each day, by my clients, meetings, deadlines, and whatever else took place within the organization that took away from my time with God and self. I realized that I don't want to ever allow anything to control me to the point that I start to lose myself and my family as I did when I went to a job that was restricting my ability to work.

God has shown me that we must be exposed, we must allow ourselves to humble down to nothing. In order to get to the place of work, we must first lose our jobs. I'm not telling folks to go out there and quit their jobs--that's not the right decision in most cases. What I'm saying is that we must not focus on a job. We must wait on God to send us to work and meditate, pray, and go within while we are on our jobs as we wait on work.

I know how desperately many of us want to get back to a job when we are unemployed. It was an everyday thought for me. I waited patiently for the phone to ring with a job offer. I posted daily on every website that was hiring. I called everybody I knew trying to find work.

It's outlandish how bad I wanted to get back to something that, many times, I didn't enjoy for long. I think about how it consumed my mind and ate at my spirit. I would think about all the things I might be missing out on because I didn't have a job. I felt like I was no longer part of a group; I felt distant and different, even a little weird and displaced. I didn't feel as though I still fit into society. In my mind, I was no longer an active, productive citizen.

But it was in this weirdness, this different state, that I had started to transform from the place I had been and realized I was losing control and going to the place God wanted me to be. I didn't care anymore about what people said or thought about me. I must admit that I used to always be a little concerned about my image and how I appeared and, suddenly, it didn't matter. To the world I appeared as an unemployed African American woman; what did that really mean--it meant nothing. I was just another number, another face at the unemployment office, and I was just another victim of a corrupt ungodly system called Capitalism.

When I started to put things into perspective, I soon realized I was on the better side of the fence. Now I could go to work; I was free. I was free from a job and open for work. I had been praying for God to close doors and open doors. Finally, I started to see He had opened doors that had been locked. Doors that even had me locked behind them. He was opening them and closing them so fast to protect me so that I could never return to that state of control. I saw that the door He wanted to open was the door to my soul. My soul was open and available. but this didn't occur totally until He locked all the doors I had hidden behind for years. I was now in a position to lose control. I didn't care what others thought about me. I was able to re-evaluate my purpose and refocus on truly living and working for Him.

It is in an out of control situation that you find yourself finding the most control available to you. The irony for me was that I found mine when I lost my control to my unseen faith. I could see everything around me and felt as though I had all this power and control. But it was when my faith was tested by the tornado that came into my world and destroyed my plans that I was able to see that I never had control. It was in the place that I discovered my lost morals, values, and the real meaning of life.

This is my journey; this is me being roasted. I know that we all have to lose our control. Even the greatest king in history, David, one of the strongest and controlled people of the Bible had to lose control; he danced all about like a wild man and in his out of control spirit, God delivered. We must understand that God will deliver when we decide to let go of our control.

Destiny and Transformation

The process of being a person of faith takes time and requires going through many ups and downs. For me, it involved trying to uncover my destiny and stepping into the position and place that God would have me proclaim.

We all have a destiny, a place, and a purpose in this world. It sometimes takes us a while to figure it out and sometimes we never know what it should even look like in order to step into the place that is prepared for us. Finding my destiny meant letting go of my past and allowing myself to open my mind to new situations, encounters, and people. I have never been one that has felt like I have to seek out my destiny, but I have never been one that has been in a place that I didn't know where I was going.

As I stated earlier, it was muddy on my windows, but it soon started to get clearer as God transformed me. He led me to a place of forgiveness and took me through the process of discovery. I'm still in the midst of my transformation; we all are in this place to some level. I know that I will never truly be transformed into what He sees in me until I'm no longer in this physical body. I'm in a process of roasting that is showing me some things within my own spirit and leading me to understand the decisions placed before me.

I'm realizing that, in order to proclaim my destiny, I have to confront the things that would hinder me on that path or cause me to fall down into a place that I would try to obtain and regain the control, only to give it over to something or someone that God did not ordain me to give my control to.

It's hard to ask to be put into a place that can be vulnerable, but God is funny like that. He has humor in His plans, and He does not always show us what He is trying to do in us when we most want Him to. We are merely pieces of clay that he has molded; we are not the ruler of our vessels. Our destiny is tied to a past that we can't wrap our mind around, a past that is unique in its own right. It's full of the sacrifice and pain that our ancestors went through for us.

Because of this sacrifice and pain, we are able to get caught up in our own control and have the freedom to live in our own state. However, we all have a will and a desire to be more and want more. I know when I started on this unemployment journey, I was optimistic and full of ambition, until weeks turned into months and months turned into years.

As the seasons changed, and they changed much during my process, I became weak. I needed more to see my destiny; I needed to have something to give me hope. I needed an awakening. I needed a change and a call to what I thought was me discovering a job.

The job that I thought I was discovering never came to be; it just became more of a daily battle not to allow this situation to define me. I realized during the challenging months and days that God still always showed up to give me a glimpse of my destiny.

I still had muddy windows, but I could see slivers of light shining through and rays of hope that inspired me to not stay idle. They charged me to go into another place of faith. It pushed me into the process of walking in my destiny and proclaiming what work I should obtain. Even when I started to proclaim my work, the phone would not ring. The application would be denied, and I would still sit with my mind twisted around the world that I once adored. The twisting of my thoughts crossed over into my spirit and tangled up into questions about the God I served.

Every time I start to try to question my situation, He shows me how truly fortunate I have been. He brings to my mind the supportive husband working hard each day, and the wonderful children that I am blessed with. He reveals to me how He had even touched hearts at the private school my kids attended to show them favor in my unfortunate situation. He opens my eyes to the beautiful house I own, the lovely car I drive, and how I had been able to pay the bills despite of my finances. When these things were placed before me, the things I didn't have or thought I needed meant nothing anymore. He started to show me that I had a destiny, that it was right in front of me, and how I needed to proclaim it and show gratitude.

I know many of us don't look at what's in front of us when we need to, but in a time when folks are dying in wars, earthquakes are destroying countries, floods are raging, and people can't afford food to eat, it started to tear at my heart for being so selfish and blinded by the destiny I should have already proclaimed and won.

When I realized all the blessings in my life, I had to stop thinking about all my misfortunes. I had stop living in the mind of a victim and proclaim the mind of a worker. I realized that all these years I had been complaining like a victim. I had been caught up in the things that folks had done to me and, although I had forgiven, I now was carrying the attitude of the victim.

Yes, I had to acknowledge that I had run into some pretty cruel and ungodly people in my work environments and everyday life, but I shouldn't let their attitudes and power keep making me a victim. I knew that I had to be bigger than that. I thought about the people I knew that really were victims: the folks that had been denied human rights, whose homes flooded, who lost all their possessions in earthquakes, who were tortured, beaten, and sometimes killed. They are victims.

My spirit may have been broken by the choices of others, however, I had never been a victim of any awful crimes. I was still alive, and I was moving forward towards my destiny. I had let go of my control and God was setting me free. I realized if those real victims of crime and devastation could move forward, I had no choice but to do the same.

I knew that I had won the hearing without even going to trial. I had won because I had stood up for all those who had sat down. I had moved in my faith, and I didn't allow the jaws of the enemy to come down and tear me to pieces. I had faced my faults, acknowledged my wrongs, and was walking into the place of my real work.

God is Fixing the Broken Parts

I realized that I can't be the victim, because in God there are no victims; we are all warriors who have answered the biggest call. We have chosen to live by our faith, trusting in a God that is unseen. We have chosen to not allow the world to label us and put us in a box so that we can't move forward. What we have chosen to do is go forth declaring victory and knowing that the battle is already won.

I had to put on my game face and shake myself out of the victim's lifestyle. The victim hides in his or her room and goes undercover because they are ashamed of what happened to them. I, at first, was ashamed. I felt broken and beat, but the spirit would always come to me and say "No, you must press on." So, I pressed on in faith, not knowing the outcome of this trial. However, I knew that at the end of the gate and sitting in the judge's stand was a God and He was going to be holding my hand.

I smiled when I pictured the strength that carried and the power infused within me and my circumstance. I saw the job was what used to align me for my destiny; I saw that the job had just prepared me to deal with scrutiny and pain. That I was not allowed to be seen, and I should not want to be seen as the victim. Because you're not the victim when you have a higher court on your side; the justice is in facing your attacker and you know that in the end, no matter what, you still win. They didn't get the best of you; they didn't kill you. Yes, they may have hindered something, but there is nothing that God can't fix.

God is now fixing the broken parts of my life. He is aligning me into the place of my destiny. Through this broken place, the victim has discovered her faith. She has discovered that beneath the tears, the pain, the weeping, the enduring, the long suffering, and the rejection, she is someone and the person that she was before is no longer. It's the dying process that the word of God speaks of. Paul mentions it when he states that "we must die daily to ourselves," in the book of Romans.

In the victim you die; you die to all the unjust things not only done to you but also that you have done to others. You die in the spirit of truth. You die as you are reconnected to your faith. Your faith is challenged, and it's restored to a new level. As you walk into this new level of faith, you realize it is here that you truly can begin to work You understand that the work is not just to go into a job and do what is demanded of you.

You realize that the work is deeper than your own self; it's the acceptance of not allowing anything outside of you to control you. It's not allowing anything to be put in front of God. When you work, you work in the spirit of blessing through your actions, your thoughts, and your deeds. When you begin to acknowledge your true boss, you realize that all others are just imposters that stand in His place. The imposters are soon eliminated by your freedom, the freedom you have found by giving up total control to the "Christ Spirit" within.

In order to be placed into the right work that God has ordained for us, we must find the place where our faith, family, love, passions, and dreams all meet and the roasting process is allowed to be completed. I know most people will think that this could never occur. I truly believe that God can take us to a place of balance. We can uncover this balance and be set free in the crazy pursuit for a job.

I have always been of the mindset that passion will lead to profit. I know that if you have passion and you love what you do, the money, the success, the love, and the balance will follow. In life we are always searching, and we will continue to search for the work. At least when we have been through the roasting process, have been able to purge ourselves from the burden of an unforgiving heart, and are able to know the love that overshadows any hurt feelings, we can begin to take that walk into work.

My life has had its share of disappointments, setbacks, trials, tribulations, changed plans, and turmoil. However, my life has also been full of love and many great experiences. I have learned to seek out and find balance within myself and focus on the positive. The balance and positive thinking becomes the key to everything in your life, which includes seeing your work revealed.

Balance continues to be found in being true to myself and realizing I can't be all things to everyone and that it's okay to be content in your situation, but to always know that it is just a temporary situation and things do and will change. I had to realize that it's not selfish to want to be happy, loved, and appreciated. You don't have to be the servant leader always trying to make others happy. We take on this spirit of always wanting to adhere to others when unfortunate situations like losing your job make you feel guilty, ashamed, and lost because you're looking for other's approval of your situation.

I had to understand that happiness comes from self and learning to sometimes say no. You have to always stay true to you and love yourself unconditionally. It is not being conceited to hold yourself in high regard; it's being convinced and sure enough of yourself that you can hold your head high despite your condition or state of affairs.

You learn to balance whatever life throws your way, whether it be good or bad. You learn to let go of situations and people that don't have your best interest at heart. You look at your position in life and you tell yourself that you can succeed.

Everyone will know that you have an anointing that you didn't ask for, and they may have prayed for but God handed it to you. We all have an anointing and it's in discovering that anointing that we find the favor of God. The anointing is when you become so consumed with being happy and basking in God's grace and love that you don't even realize what's truly underneath your anointing. Underneath that anointing is misery and pain that came out of struggles and learning to walk in the "Christ Spirit."

You finally wake up and grasp that these unfortunate occurrences are not mere coincidences but divine intervention and blessings to anoint you with a favor you could have never imagined possible while going through your grief. You understand that you have a purpose, and you realize that the purpose has been standing right in front of you yelling out your name.

You come to a place of knowledge and you accept that it is the balance of your faith and forgiveness that brings you closer to your work, and you live life everyday like it is a journey to be taken and a road to be shared and crossed. You look at life as if it is a path you must go down and, as you walk on this journey, you notice side trails placed to throw you off course and lakes you must learn to swim. However, you realize that in connecting to your faith you will always be guided down the right road.

Through it all you learn to understand that life is to be lived and to be celebrated and enjoyed, and every small victory is a win in your favor. You accept that you must never consume all the control ever again because when you do you start to walk away from your work. When you walk away from your work, your life will truly become unbalanced, and your faith will be tried.

I have decided not to worry about a job but to start to pray for my work and give gratitude. I live and recognize life for what it is: it is to be lived. I understand that I have so much more to give. For me, life is the simple things, the little small treats we sometimes forget to share. It's the love of wine, a good book, it's the things we sometimes forget to hold onto like the cuddle of my husband, holding his hand, or the giggles of my kids, sitting with my girlfriends over a delicious meal, dancing in the rain, or just meditating on love. It's those things we can't put into a jar and savor, but if we could, we'd keep them all in a treasure box forever.

It's no longer about a job when you have decided to let the Lord give you work. You now have to endure to the end and just wait on him--yet again. You learn to trust in your faith and to stand strong on his word, because outside of a job is the work that needs to be done. So, you are thankful for the small things, grateful for the big things, and you learn to be content with everything in between and find a way to balance as He continues to will your life into His work.

Acknowledgments

I want to acknowledge my tribes and all those who have been a part of this journey with me. There are so many that influenced me through the years and have been my backbone when I was weak.

I'm so grateful for my family, my siblings Stephanie, Louis Jr, aka Woo, and all my cousins who are more like siblings. Y'all know who you are! I thank you for always being there when I needed a word of encouragement, for being my cheerleaders, and for just showing me love.

First, I'd like to acknowledge Pastor Jamal Bryant for his inspiring sermon that day. Your words touched my soul and summonsed me to seek the face of God for my work. The day I turned on your sermon was a dark day for me. I was depressed and contemplating suicide. I never thought I would get that low, but that day I was truly down.

Thank you, Kamilah, my friend who posted the sermon. I know that this was all divine and a part of God's plan. If you had not posted that sermon, I'm not sure where I would be at this moment. I know people think Facebook can be evil, but that day Facebook saved my life, so Thank you, Mark Zuckerberg, for giving us a platform to share.

Thank you, Amanda and Moneeka for bringing my vision together and Faith Blackwell for capturing me in this cover picture. I also acknowledge my All Saints childhood tribe Chrise, Hope, Lacretia, Mary, and T

Nicole, aka Mook, for being my sisters and always showing me love. You have inspired me in more ways than you know.

Finally, there are so many to acknowledge, from my sands to my Cardinal Ritter crew Anita, Cindy, Lauri, Lucia, and so many more who have cheered me on each day. If I did not mention you, please do not take offense. I appreciate you too. However, these are the ones that lifted me during this dark time and were there, in the beginning, to cheer me on when I was so down.

I thank all those who continue to pour into me each day, and I pray that I encourage and pour into you all as much as you have all poured into me. May you be blessed by the words in this book and find your work.

About the Author

Tiffany Thompson is an author, actress, counselor, educator, model, and owner of Cre8tive Recovery, LLC, a counseling and consulting company. She specializes in using expressive therapies, the open studio process, mindfulness, and other holistic therapeutic approaches for whole-body healing.

She is currently working on her doctorate in Expressive Therapies at Lesley University in Cambridge, Massachusetts. In addition, Tiffany has a certificate in dance therapy, professional background, and a degree in Performance Theater.

Additionally, she is an adjunct for Indiana University -Purdue University, where she teaches play and expressive therapies courses for Herron College and Counseling/Counselor Education College. She also writes a monthly counseling blog for a local youth magazine called Boldly U.

She has presented and sat on a panel at Nagindas Khandwala College in Mumbai, India, to discuss professional identity and advocacy skills development promoting creative arts therapy techniques with culturally diverse populations. In addition, she recently presented for the Creative Movement Therapy Association in India on Reaching Children Exposed to trauma in the school through expressive therapies. She advocates for using culturally aware practices and is passionate about helping clients who have experienced trauma connect to the whole person using spiritual principles, empathy, and the arts.

As an advocate for social justice, she frequently works with youth organizations. In addition, she has written several children's books, including *Mindfulness and Me, The Blessed Arm, My Upside Down Reading Made Write,* and *Finding My Zen.*

Tiffany resides in Indianapolis, Indiana, with her husband Curtis, sons Noble, Bryce, Logan, and their mini-sheepadoodle Schroeder.

Connect

with the Author

Website: www.cre8tiverecovery.com

Facebook: Cre8tive Recovery, LLC

Instagram: @cre8tiverecovery

Creative Control With Self-Publishing

Divine Legacy Publishing provides authors with the guid-ance necessary to take creative control of their work through self-publishing. We provide:

Writing Coaching

Professional Editing

Author Branding

Self-Publishing Coaching

Graphic Design

Website Design

Let Divine Legacy Publishing help you master the business of self-publishing.

Made in the USA
Columbia, SC
24 January 2025

52402001R00062